LOOKING AT ANIMALS WITH MR. ETCH A SKETCH®

Written by

Edna Cucksey Stephens

and

Diane Norberg Farstvedt

Best Wishes Always,
Tim George

Etch A Sketch® illustrations by Tim George

Cover and page design by **Mark J. Herrick**

Tim George photograph ©2002 **Barbara Schwartz Photography** - Used with permission

Animal photographs courtesy of **Michigan Department of Natural Resources** - **David Kenyon**, Photographer

Etch A Sketch® is a registered trademark of **The Ohio Art Company** - Used with permission

MAGIC Etch A Sketch® SCREEN

Book published by...

EDCO Publishing Inc.

2648 Lapeer Rd.
Auburn Hills, MI 48326
(248) 475-4678
Fax (248) 475-9122
www.edcopublishing.com

For Mom, my four sisters: Martha, Kaye, Faye and Lois and five brothers:
Stanley, Donnie, Scotty, Clint and Ricky
E.C.S.

For Jerry, John, Julie, Mom and Dad
D.N.F.

For Ellie: Your courage and determination have always been an inspiration.
You made it possible for me to discover my artistic side.
T.G.

Thanks to Frank Boster for photographs of Tim George's Etch A Sketch™ drawings.

Special thanks to Lynette Post

Text Copyright ©2002 Edna Cucksey Stephens
Poems Copyright ©2002 Diane Norberg Farstvedt
Etch A Sketch® art Copyright ©2002 Tim George
Animal photographs Copyright ©2002 Michigan Department of Natural Resources. Used with permission.

Etch A Sketch® is a registered trademark of The Ohio Art Company. All rights reserved. Used with permission.

EDCO Publishing, Inc.,
2648 Lapeer Road
Auburn Hills, Michigan 48326
www.edcopublishing.com

Printed in the United States of America
First Printing 2002

10 9 8 7 6 5 4 3 2

Paperback ISBN 0-9712692-1-1

A portion of the proceeds from this book will benefit the Michigan Department of Natural Resources' Outdoor Explorers Club for kids.

MAGIC *Etch A Sketch* SCREEN

Table of Contents

JUST FOR FUN

How do bears walk?
On bare feet

What would you get if you crossed a small bear and a skunk?
Winnie the Phew

Bears can be a problem around open dumps. When bears lose their fear of humans they become more dangerous.

BLACK BEAR

Big and round the black bears roam
Looking for a woodland home.

They find a log and cave to rest.
This den will make a perfect nest.

They sleep and may wake up to eat,
Bugs and berries, fish and meat.

And then, upon a springtime morn-
A pair of twins! Bear cubs are born!

Bears can run at speeds of 25-30 miles per hour.

The helmets of Great Britain's Buckingham Palace guards are made of black bear fur.

Bears love honey and will rip open a beehive to get it. Its thick coat protects it from bee stings.

YOUNG

Black bears have 1-2 babies, every other year. They are called cubs and are 8 inches long and weigh 7 or 8 ounces. They are born with pink skin and no hair. The mother feeds them in their den until spring. She cares for the cubs until they are 18 months old.

HABITAT AND OTHER FACTS

Black bears usually live alone in wooded areas, forests or swamps. Sometimes they live near suburban areas where they can find food in the garbage dumps. Most active at dawn or dusk, bears mark the trees with their scent and fur. Logs and hornets' or bees' nests that have been torn apart are signs that a bear has been there. Their dens may be in caves, hollow trees or logs. Bears are not true hibernators. They are called "light sleepers" because they often wake up to eat on warmer winter days.

The sign said, "No fishing allowed," so the bear fished silently.

CHARACTERISTICS

Black bears have long black, light brown or reddish fur. They are about 4 1/2 to 6 feet long and weigh 250 to 300 pounds. Bears are nocturnal animals, although they can be seen during the day. They have a clumsy walk, are good swimmers and can climb trees. Bears live to be about 15 to 30 years old. Predators of black bears include cougars and wolves.

FOOD

Black bears eat both meat and plants. Although they are big and powerful, their diet includes mostly small items. They eat ants, crickets, beetles, grubs, nuts, berries, mice and other small mammals, fish, honey, roots, bark, twigs, leaves, carrion (dead animals) and garbage.

JUST FOR FUN

One Sunday a beaver started to swim ashore, then turned and went back to his lodge. Why didn't he go ashore?

The banks are closed on Sunday.

What did the beaver say to the tree?

It's been nice gnawing (knowing) you.

During fur trading years, beavers were trapped for their thick fur.

BEAVER

There once was a pond in the wood.
A beaver thought this spot was good
To build him a home
In the shape of a dome,
So he gnawed all the trees that he could.

And soon the trees fell with a thud.
Dragged to water, he packed them in mud.
He piled them high,
And soon by and by,
The pond water started to flood.

Friends eagerly came to his aid.
They started a building brigade.
They gnawed and they swam
As they worked on the dam,
And in no time a great home
was made.

Beavers do not hibernate over winter, but they will stay in their lodge, where they have stored enough food to last until spring.

Beavers cannot move very quickly on land. If danger is near they head to the water and go into their lodge.

Beavers are strong swimmers. They swim up to 5 miles per hour. They can hold their breath for 15 minutes under water.

YOUNG

Beavers have 3-5 babies at a time, called kits. Kits have thick dark fur and weigh one pound. They are able to swim 30 minutes after birth. The kits are nursed by their mother for 8-10 weeks. She carries them on her back, tail or in her front paws when they go out of the lodge. They can care for themselves after two years.

HABITAT AND OTHER FACTS

Beavers live near fresh water and trees. Some homes are lodges inside a dam, using sticks, stones and mud to form a dome-shaped shelf above the water. Others make burrows with an underwater entrance in the riverbank. They are nocturnal animals, most active a night. Beavers are always cutting and hauling trees, building dams and repairing their work. They are "busy beavers."

CHARACTERISTICS

Beavers are 3 feet long with large, flat tails and weigh 30 to 70 pounds. They spend much of their time in water. Beavers have webbed feet, ear and nostril flaps and clear eyelids that close when under water. Predators of beavers include the otter, gray wolf, coyote, red fox and bobcat.

FOOD

Beavers eat tree bark, leaves, buds, fruit, ferns, roots, twigs and water plants. Their large orange teeth would continue to grow if they were not worn down by gnawing on trees. The trees are used to build dams and lodges. Beavers chew down hundreds of trees each year. Branches are eaten or stored underwater to be used for food during winter months.

5

JUST FOR FUN

What fur do you get from a bobcat?

As fur away as you can get

What makes a female bobcat happy?

When she gets a mink

What always follows a bobcat when it travels?

Its tail

Bobcats can run up to 30 miles an hour.

BOBCAT

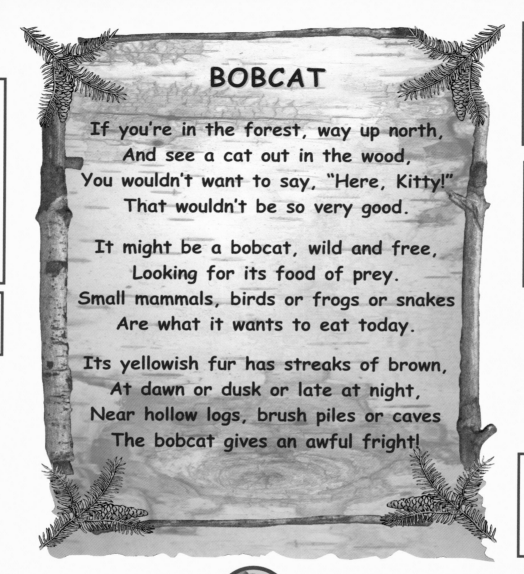

If you're in the forest, way up north,
And see a cat out in the wood,
You wouldn't want to say, "Here, Kitty!"
That wouldn't be so very good.

It might be a bobcat, wild and free,
Looking for its food of prey.
Small mammals, birds or frogs or snakes
Are what it wants to eat today.

Its yellowish fur has streaks of brown,
At dawn or dusk or late at night,
Near hollow logs, brush piles or caves
The bobcat gives an awful fright!

Bobcats have excellent vision and hearing. They use these senses when hunting. Soft padded feet help them sneak up on their prey.

Bobcats usually sound like a house cat, but can scream or yowl. They make a loud cough-bark sound when they are afraid.

At one time, bobcats were disappearing because of unregulated trapping. Now, their numbers are increasing.

YOUNG

Bobcats have two or three babies in a litter and are born blind. Baby bobcats are called kittens. They have spotted fur at birth. The kittens are fed by their mother for two months. Then they can hunt on their own, but stay with their mother until they are a year old. Predators of young bobcats are foxes and owls.

HABITAT AND OTHER FACTS

Bobcats live in forests and marshlands. They make their dens under fallen logs, in the roots of fallen trees or in big cracks in rocks. Their den is lined with a nest of leaves for the birth of kittens. Sometimes they can be seen resting on boulders or on low tree branches. Bobcats are nocturnal because the animals they hunt are most active at night. They follow the same paths when hunting their prey.

CHARACTERISTICS

Bobcats are wild cats. They are about two feet tall and weigh about 20 pounds. They have dark streaks in their yellow-gray coat with a ruff of fur on the sides of their face. Bobcats are named for their stubby "bobbed" tail. They are shy and spend much time alone. Bobcats do not usually bother people. Their worst enemies are hunters and cars.

FOOD

Bobcats stalk their prey and pounce on it, leaping up to 10 feet. They are fast and powerful hunters and often kill their prey with one powerful bite of their sharp teeth. Bobcats' diet includes rabbits, mice, squirrels, minks, woodchucks, opossums, muskrats, skunks, foxes, porcupines, birds, bats, snakes, frogs, small deer and carrion (dead animals).

JUST FOR FUN

How do deer start a race?

Ready-set-doe!

What did the deer say when he sailed off on a cruise?

Antlers aweigh!

What did the buck say when the doe said, "Let's go out for dinner tonight"?

"Yes, Deer!"

Male deer are called bucks, female deer are called does and baby deer are called fawns.

WHITE-TAILED DEER

Gentle doe, quiet buck,
Spotted little fawn,
Forest, swamps, meadow lands,
Seen at dusk and dawn.

Antlers high, watchful eyes,
Careful listening ear.
Tail goes up, leaping high,
Enemies are near.

A raised tail is a signal to the other deer that danger is near.

Deer can be found in groups of up to 25 and can run up to 40 miles per hour.

Deer have a good sense of smell, keen hearing and eyesight, but they are color-blind.

YOUNG

White-tailed deer have 1-2 babies each year. Baby deer, called fawns, are light brown with white spots. They weigh 5-8 pounds. Their mother nurses them for 4 months. When fawns are a couple of weeks old they also begin eating plants. Males (bucks) care for themselves after one year. Females (does) are on their own after 2 years.

HABITAT AND OTHER FACTS

The white-tailed deer can be found in farmlands, brushy areas, woods, suburbs and gardens. They nest by making a space in hidden grassy areas. They are most active at dusk and dawn. White-tailed deer are the most popular big game animal in North America. Hunting helps keep the deer population in balance with its food supply. Without hunting, many deer would starve to death.

MAGIC Etch·A·Sketch® SCREEN

8

YOUNG

White-tailed deer are tan or reddish brown in summer and grayish brown in winter. The belly, throat, nose, eye ring, inside of ears and underside of the tail are white. Does weigh about 85-130 pounds and bucks weigh 100-300 pounds. Bucks have antlers up to 3 feet wide that are shed each winter. Predators of deer are wolves, coyotes, ears, bobcats, cougars and humans.

FOOD

White-tailed deer eat mostly plants. Their diet includes twigs, leaves, grasses, wildflowers, mushrooms, bark, fruits and nuts. Deer are grazers and nibblers, moving from one food to another. Although it is unusual, they have been known to eat snails and fish.

9

JUST FOR FUN

If 5 foxes catch 5 mice in 5 minutes, how long would it take one fox to catch one mouse?

5 minutes

What is a fox after it is 3 years old?

Four years old

Why did the fox cross the road?

It was after that darned chicken.

RED FOX

This super little athlete
Can run and leap and swim.
The fields and forests,
ponds and streams
Have food and homes for him.

His fur is sleek and shiny.
His bushy tail is long.
He's sly when hunting, but he runs
When bobcats come along.

Foxes can run at speeds up to 30 mph and are excellent swimmers.

A fox's hearing is so good it can hear its prey digging, gnawing or rustling underground.

Red foxes were imported from England to be hunted for sport.

A red fox can leap 15 feet in a single bound, three times farther than a kangaroo.

YOUNG

Red foxes have 5-10 babies in a litter. The babies, called kits, weigh 3-8 ounces each. They are born gray, with a white-tipped tail. After nursing for 10 weeks, the mother and other adult foxes chew food and feed it to the kits. Soon the mother brings live prey so the kits can learn to hunt. At 7 months the kits go off to live on their own.

HABITAT AND OTHER FACTS

Red foxes live in open fields near woodlands and fresh water. They can be seen curled up with their tails, called sweeps, wrapped around them. Their sweeps help to keep them warm. Foxes make their dens in tree roots, woodpiles or empty woodchuck burrows. They also make underground dens to have their babies. Foxes are nocturnal, but may be seen at dawn or dusk. They are cautious and shy and like to travel alone.

MAGIC Etch A Sketch SCREEN

CHARACTERISTICS

Red foxes can be many colors from rusty red to black, silver and dark brown. All foxes have white undersides and bushy black-tipped tails. An average red fox is 20-40 inches long and weighs 8-15 pounds. It has a sleek body. Predators of red foxes are bobcats, coyotes and humans.

FOOD

Red foxes stalk their prey, sneak up as close as possible, then bolt. They continue to hunt even when full, and bury the catch for later. They eat mice, eggs, birds, worms, insects, frogs, lizards, rabbits, squirrels, woodchucks, fish and carrion (dead animals). In summer, foxes also eat corn, grass, nuts, berries, apples, cherries and grapes.

11

JUST FOR FUN

What does a moose wear for a disguise?

A fake moostache

What do you call a very large moose?

Enor-moose

Where do you get kissed by a moose?

Under the moosle toe

MOOSE

An animal strolled through the wood.
And got closer to me than he should.
Is a moose on the loose?
I can only deduce
That this state of affairs isn't good!

I know that his eyesight is bad.
I don't know how much food he has had-
But I'm not a tree,
So he wouldn't eat me,
I just hope that he doesn't get mad!

His antlers would make quite a rack.
He stands five feet tall at his back.
Wait! I think I see him
Going in for a swim-
Now I won't be afraid
of attack!

The antlers of a bull moose are shed in the winter. A new set of antlers begin to grow in March.

Under the neck of a male moose there is some hair which is called a dewlap or a bell. The bell looks like a beard.

A moose is heavier than four refrigerators.

Moose are the largest members of the deer family. The word moose is a Native American word that means, "twig eater".

YOUNG

Moose have 1-2 babies called calves in late spring. Calves weigh 25-35 pounds. They have reddish-brown fur. Calves are nursed by their mothers for one year. They are then chased off before new calves are born. Predators of young moose are cougars and coyotes.

HABITAT AND OTHER FACTS

Moose live in dense, soggy wooded areas, spruce forests, swamps and aspen and willow thickets. They make their nesting areas in brushy, trampled vegetation. Moose like to be alone, but will gather in herds in the winter because the packed snow makes movement easier. They may gather with others near streams and lakes to feed. Moose can swim for miles and almost as fast as two people can paddle a canoe.

MAGIC *Etch A Sketch* SCREEN

—Tim George

CHARACTERISTICS

A moose has four long, skinny legs, a drooping nose and a tiny tail. Moose are about 7-10 feet long and weigh 800-1800 pounds. They have dark brown to black fur. Their antlers, called palmate, are shaped like the palm of your hand. A palmate can grow to 5 or 6 feet across. Moose can live to be 20 years old. Predators of adult moose include man, bears and wolves.

FOOD

Moose eat plants and trees, especially birch, aspen, dogwood, maple, cherry and willow. Moose can pack up to 50 pounds of leaves, twigs, stems and bark each day in their four stomachs. Excellent swimmers, they will often dive as deep as 18 feet to pull plants from the bottom of a pond. Then they float tail-first to the surface while munching.

13

JUST FOR FUN

What animal is the best actor in the woods?

Opossum - he plays dead.

Why did the chicken cross the road?

To prove to the opossum that it could be done.

Who are the only ones that think an opossum is beautiful?

Other opossums

OPOSSUM

He has a pouch like kangaroos,
Hangs upside down like bats.
His tracks are almost like raccoons.
His tail is like the rats.

His white face has a long pink snout.
Like birds, wants worms to eat.
He eats all night like porcupines,
Like buzzards, eats dead meat.

He's like a lot of animals,
But none are quite the same.
And he's unique when he plays dead.
Opossum is his name.

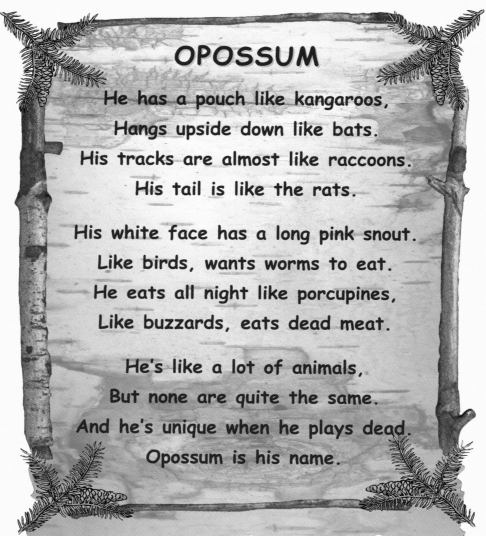

Opossums hiss, screech, slobber and show all of their 50 teeth in order to scare away their enemies.

Opossums are called living fossils because they look the same as they did a million years ago.

Opossums use their tails as a fifth limb. Their tails help them hang upside down in trees.

When threatened, opossums may roll over, shut their eyes, and let their tongues hang out, playing dead or "playing possum" for up to three hours.

YOUNG

Opossums have 6-20 babies, called kits, in a litter. Kits are one half inch long and weigh less than one ounce; the size of a bee. When born, the hairless kits crawl into their mother's pouch. They nurse for 8 weeks. Then the kits ride on the mother's back until they are 12 weeks old.

HABITAT AND OTHER FACTS

Opossums live in wooded areas and farmland near water. They do not make nests. They are comfortable both on the ground and in trees. In winter they rest in empty burrows and hollow trees. Opossums like to live alone. They are nocturnal and hunt for food just after sunset and just before dawn. Opossums' tails often get frost-bitten because they have no hair on them for protection.

MAGIC *Etch A Sketch* SCREEN

Tim George

CHARACTERISTICS

Opossums are rat-like animals with grayish white fur and no hair on their ears and tail. They have a white face with a long, pink snout. Opossums are 13-20 inches long with a 9-15 inch tail. They weigh 4-15 pounds. They are North America's only native marsupials, meaning they have a kangaroo-like pouch where the babies stay until fully developed. Predators include bobcats, coyotes, foxes, hawks and owls.

FOOD

Opossums eat almost everything. They have 50 teeth, more than any other land mammal in North America. Their diet includes worms, reptiles, eggs, grain, garbage, insects, mice, moles, snakes, frogs, apples, berries, corn and carrion (dead animals).

JUST FOR FUN

What would you get if you crossed a porcupine and a young goat?

A stuck-up kid

What did the porcupine say to the cactus?

Is that you, Mama?

What do porcupines say when they hug?

OUCH!

PORCUPINE

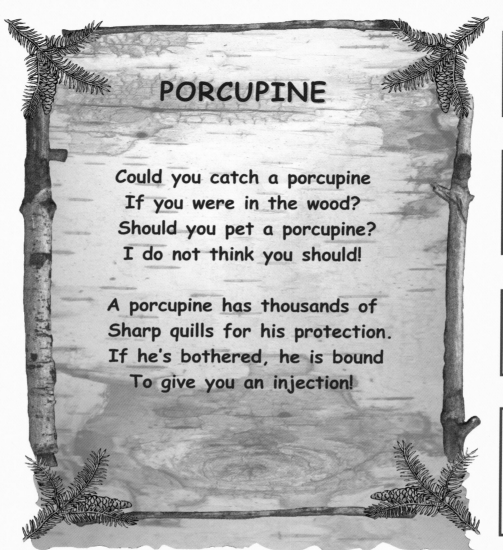

Could you catch a porcupine
If you were in the wood?
Should you pet a porcupine?
I do not think you should!

A porcupine has thousands of
Sharp quills for his protection.
If he's bothered, he is bound
To give you an injection!

Native Americans used porcupine quills for decorations.

A porcupine will defend itself by swinging its tail or jumping in order to stick its sharp quills into its enemy.

A porcupine cannot throw its quills at an enemy, as some believe.

A porcupine's front teeth are orange and continue to grow throughout its life, so it must gnaw on hard objects to wear the teeth down.

YOUNG

Porcupines have one baby at a time in the late spring. Baby porcupines, called porcupettes or pups, are born with dark fur and weigh one pound. They have soft one inch quills. The pups usually live in a hollow log and are nursed by their mothers for 3 months. They can care for themselves when they are about five months old.

HABITAT AND OTHER FACTS

Porcupines live in forests and dry, scrubby areas with scattered trees. They make their dens in hollow logs, tree cavities, under stumps and buildings, in caves and in abandoned burrows of other animals. Porcupines are nocturnal, which means they are most active at night. They spend their days resting in trees. Porcupines like to live alone.

MAGIC Etch A Sketch SCREEN

Tim George

CHARACTERISTICS

Porcupines are chunky rodents with a high-arching back, short legs and 30,000 quills on its rump and tail. An average porcupine is about 26 to 37 inches long, with a 6-11 inch tail. They weigh 7 to 40 pounds and live to be about 7 or 8 years old. Porcupines have strong, sharp, curved claws that help them climb trees to get food and are also used for grooming. Predators include the fisher, mountain lion, bobcat and coyote.

FOOD

Porcupines climb trees to eat bark, leaves, twigs, evergreen needles, nuts, acorns and fruit. In the winter they damage trees as they strip away the bark. Their diet also includes clover, grass and seeds. Porcupines like salt and will even eat leather boots and the handles of wooden tools to get the salt left by sweaty hands.

JUST FOR FUN

What would you get if you crossed a rabbit with a frog?

A bunny ribbit

What would you get if you crossed an insect with a rabbit?

Bugs Bunny

There are about 25 different kinds of rabbits.

RABBIT

Have you ever heard rabbits?
No, they're quite a quiet bunch.
But you're sure to hear rabbits,
Eating vegetables for lunch!

Have you ever seen a rabbit,
With long ears and hair so furry?
Have you seen his little cotton tail
When he is in a hurry?

Although cottontail rabbits have great eyesight and speed, it is the most preyed-upon animal in North America.

Rabbits don't sweat.

A group of rabbit burrows is called a warren.

A female rabbit is a doe.
A male rabbit is a buck.
A baby rabbit is a kitten.

YOUNG

Rabbits have a litter of 4-7 babies every 2 to 3 months. Baby rabbits, called kittens, are born in an underground nest made of plants and fur from their mothers' chest. The kittens are 4 inches long, weigh 1 ounce and are born without fur. They are nursed for 4 weeks.

HABITAT AND OTHER FACTS

Rabbits are seen in pastures, open woodlands and near wetlands. Their homes are burrows in meadows or at the base of trees. They are nocturnal, but are often seen at dawn or dusk, or on dark days. In the winter they sometimes make a network of tunnels in the brush under the snow.

MAGIC *Etch A Sketch* SCREEN

18

How do you write the word rabbit without using an "r"?

Bunny

CHARACTERISTICS

Cottontail rabbits have grayish brown fur and a cottony white tail. They are about 14-18 inches long and weigh 2-4 pounds. Rabbits usually hop, but have been known to leap 10-15 feet. They live to be about 10 years old. Predators of rabbits include hawks, owls, dogs, foxes, raccoons, weasels, bobcats, coyotes, wolves, lynxes, falcons and eagles.

FOOD

Rabbits like to eat alfalfa, dandelion, clover, berries and garden crops in the summer. In the winter, rabbits eat tree bark, twigs and shrubs. They can often be seen feeding at sunrise and sunset.

JUST FOR FUN

What kind of jewelry does a
raccoon wear?

Rings on his tail

Why is it hard to identify a
raccoon?

It's wearing a mask.

During the fur trading era, the
fur of the raccoon was second
highest in demand after beaver
pelts. Today, some people still
wear winter coats made or
trimmed with raccoon fur.

RACCOON

Who's peeking from that hollow log?
Who's there, behind that mask?
I wonder if it is a thief.
I shouldn't have to ask!

The black-masked face should tell me
That his tail is ringed and furry.
When the raccoon comes out to eat,
Mice, bugs and crayfish
scurry!

In 1612, Captain John Smith
wrote about the raccoon
in his journal. He may have
played a part in giving the
raccoon its name.

The name raccoon comes from
the *Algonquin* Native American
word arakun and means "one
who scratches with his hands."

Raccoons are excellent
climbers and swimmers.

Raccoons have hand-like front
paws, and contrary to popular
belief, they DO NOT wash
everything they eat!

YOUNG

Raccoons have 2-7 babies in a litter. Baby
raccoons, called kits, are four inches long and
weigh about two ounces. They have light fur, a faint mask
around their eyes and a ringed tail. The kits stay in the
den until they are ten weeks old. They are nursed until
they can live on their own at 4-6 months old.

HABITAT AND OTHER FACTS

Raccoons live in wooded areas near open fields, riverbanks
and ponds. Their dens are in the hollows of standing trees,
under buildings and in abandoned woodchuck burrows. Raccoons
are nocturnal. They hunt for food at night. They sometimes raid
garbage cans and campsites. Raccoons often spend their days
sunbathing in trees.

MAGIC Etch A Sketch SCREEN

TimGeorge.

CHARACTERISTICS

Raccoons have heavy fur streaked with brown, black and gray. They have black face masks and bushy ringed tails. Raccoon are about 32 inches long including the tail and weigh 11 to 18 pounds. The largest raccoon ever recorded was over 60 pounds! Raccoons live about seven years. Predators of raccoons are coyotes, foxes and bobcats.

FOOD

Raccoons eat both plants and animals. Their diet includes frogs, turtles, crayfish, fish, birds, eggs, mice, fruits, berries, nuts, garden vegetables and insects. They have often been called black-masked scavengers because they eat carrion (dead animals) and garbage. Before winter, raccoons eat a lot and store fat to survive when less food is available.

OMNIVORE

21

JUST FOR FUN

What should you do if you find a skunk in your tent?

Sleep somewhere else

How do you stop a skunk from smelling?

Hold his nose

What do skunks have that no other animals have?

Baby skunks

SKUNK

Can a skunk be a friend?
Why, yes it can!
A skunk can be a friend to man!

Is he really a friend?
What makes him nice?
A skunk eats pesky bugs and mice!

With his shiny black coat
And bold white stripe,
He hunts for food all through the night.

If a skunk is our friend,
Then why the fuss?
When he is scared,
he sprays at us!

Spotted skunks do handstands before they spray.

A skunk will not bite and spray its scent at the same time.

A skunk is an unusual mammal because it does not blend in with its environment.

A skunk helps humans by hunting grubs, mice, moles and bugs.

YOUNG

Skunks have 5-7 babies in a litter. The baby skunks, called kits, are born in an underground den. They are wrinkled and toothless and weigh 7 ounces. The kits nurse from their mother for 6-7 weeks. Then the mother skunk begins to teach the kits to hunt. They can hunt alone when they are 10 weeks old. Mother skunks are very protective of their young and will spray if danger is near.

HABITAT AND OTHER FACTS

Skunks are found in deserts, woodlands, grassy plains and suburbs. Their dens are in wooded areas in burrows, hollow logs or under buildings and woodpiles. Skunks are nocturnal and are more often smelled than seen. Mothballs sprinkled on the ground can keep skunks from digging for insects or grubs in lawns or from entering campsites. Baby skunks can be seen walking along single file behind their mother.

MAGIC Etch A Sketch SCREEN

Tim George

CHARACTERISTICS

It's easy to spot a skunk by their shiny black fur and white stripe or spots. Skunks are are about 15 inches long with bushy, 8 inch tails. They weigh 3-10 pounds. If afraid, skunks will hiss, stomp and wave their tails. If the danger is still there, they lift their tails and spray a smelly, long-lasting liquid up to 15 feet. The strong odor can be smelled a mile away. Predators are great-horned owls and the bobcats.

FOOD

Skunks are nocturnal and search for food at night. Their diet includes insects, grubs, mice and other small mammals, bird eggs, amphibians, grasshoppers, crickets, earthworms, butterfly and moth larvae, spiders, snails, bees, wasps, honey, ants, crayfish, fruits and garbage. Skunks' long claws help them dig for food in the ground.

OMNIVORE

23

JUST FOR FUN

How does a nut feel when a squirrel chews on it?

¡poo6 os ʇnN

What does a boy squirrel say to a girl squirrel?

¡noʎ ʇnoqɐ sʇnu ɯ,I

In the spring, squirrels tear off the bark of maple trees to suck the sweet sap.

SQUIRREL

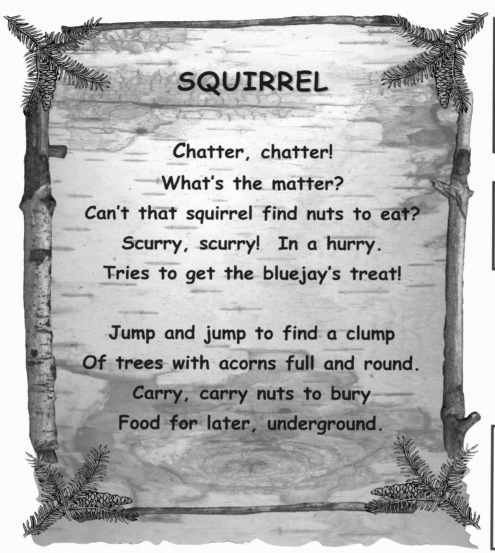

Chatter, chatter!
What's the matter?
Can't that squirrel find nuts to eat?
Scurry, scurry! In a hurry.
Tries to get the bluejay's treat!

Jump and jump to find a clump
Of trees with acorns full and round.
Carry, carry nuts to bury
Food for later, underground.

Squirrels seem to play as they jump from branch to branch. They are actually telling other squirrels to keep away from their food and den.

Mother squirrels guard their nests and will move their babies if there is danger.

Squirrels can smell a nut buried beneath 12" of snow. In the winter, they build tunnels under the snow to connect their piles of food.

YOUNG

Squirrels have a litter of 2-3 babies twice a year. The baby squirrels, called pups, weigh only 1/2 ounce and are born without hair. The winter babies are nursed by their mother for 8 weeks in a den in the hollow of a tree. The summer litter is born in a treetop nest of leaves, twigs and bark in the shape of a ball. At 12 weeks the babies can live on their own.

HABITAT AND OTHER FACTS

Squirrels live wherever there are trees. They are seen in city parks, suburbs and wooded rural areas. Some squirrels make their homes in 12-19 inch ball-shaped nests high in the branches of tree tops. Some squirrels nest in the hollows of trees.

MAGIC *Etch A Sketch* SCREEN

Tim George

CHARACTERISTICS

Squirrels are mostly gray with white undersides. Their big bushy tails help them keep their balance while jumping from branch to branch. They are about 8-11 inches long and weigh 1 1/2 pounds. Squirrels store nuts in hollow trees or bury them underground. Predators of squirrels are bears, bobcats, coyotes, wolves and hawks.

FOOD

Squirrels mainly eat nuts, seeds, fruits, buds and tree bark. They also eat insects and bird eggs. They store extra food by burying it 3-4 inches underground to use later. Squirrels can hide 25 nuts in half an hour. They can usually find 4 out of 5 of the nuts they have buried.

JUST FOR FUN

What does a wolf have in common with playing cards?

They both come in packs.

Where do wolves stay when they travel?

At a Howl-o-day Inn

Why did the wolf howl?

You would too if you had to eat mice and bugs for dinner.

Wolves can travel great distances in a short time. They can maintain a "dog-trot" for up to 20 hours without stopping.

GRAY WOLF

A single solitary wolf

Sits on a rock and howls at the sky.

A pair of gray wolves lift their ears

To hear the howl six miles away.

Six playful fuzzy young wolf pups

Romp and bite at black-tipped tails.

A pack of hungry stalking wolves

Begin to run to catch their prey.

A mother wolf nudges cubs

To their den in a hillside burrow.

The gray wolf pack with restful eyes,

Will sleep until the break of day.

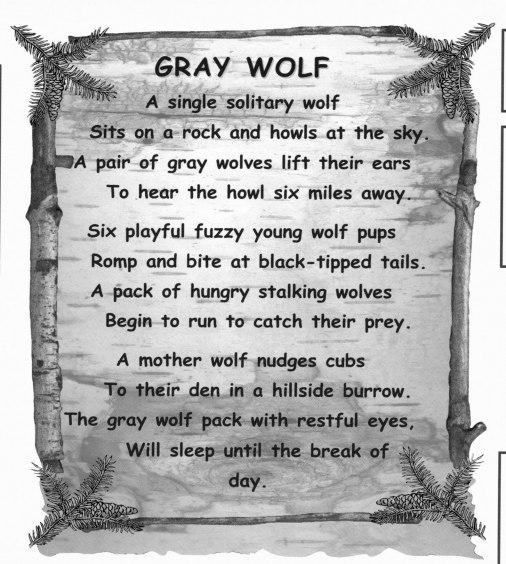

Many years ago, man tamed the wolf and it became the first dog.

Wolves are usually afraid of people. Only three attacks on humans by wolves have been documented in North America and no one died from those attacks.

A large wolf pack's territory covers 100 to 260 square miles. If there is enough food, a pack may use the same range for many years.

YOUNG

Wolves have 4-6 babies in a litter. Baby wolves, called pups, weigh about one pound at birth. The pups stay in their den and nurse for about 6 weeks. Then they can go out of the den, but their mothers chew meat for them to eat until they are about 10 weeks old. The whole pack helps to care for the pups.

HABITAT AND OTHER FACTS

Wolves live in forests. They normally do not use a shelter, but curl their tails over their noses and paws to keep warm. When having babies, the lead female digs a den in the ground or finds a burrow made by a badger or woodchuck. Although they are most active during the day, wolves sometimes hunt at night. They hunt and travel in packs of 6 to 12.

MAGIC *Etch A Sketch* SCREEN

The strongest male of a pack is normally the leader and is known as the alpha male.

CHARACTERISTICS

Wolves have fur in shades of gray, with brown, black, red or white. Their bushy black-tipped tails are 13 to 19 inches long. An average wolf is about 40 to 52 inches long and weighs 57 to 130 pounds. Wolves are best known for their howling. They live 10-18 years. Humans are wolves only important predator.

FOOD

CARNIVORE

Wolves hunt mostly at night. The pack works together to stalk and kill their prey. Their diet includes deer, beaver, rabbit, mice, moles, chipmunks, squirrels and other small animals. Wolves also eat insects, nuts, berries and grasses. They are able to eat 20 pounds of meat in a single meal, but can go without eating for a week or more.

27

JUST FOR FUN

What kind of animal does a woodchuck eat?

A dandelion

How much wood would a woodchuck chuck if a woodchuck could chuck wood?

He would chuck as much wood as a woodchuck could if a woodchuck could chuck wood.

WOODCHUCK

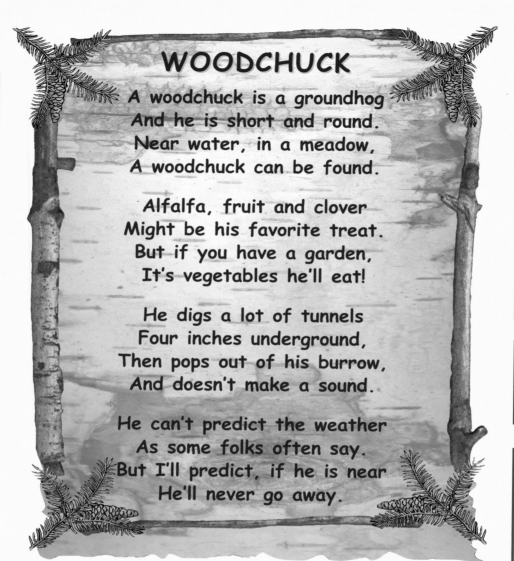

A woodchuck is a groundhog
And he is short and round.
Near water, in a meadow,
A woodchuck can be found.

Alfalfa, fruit and clover
Might be his favorite treat.
But if you have a garden,
It's vegetables he'll eat!

He digs a lot of tunnels
Four inches underground,
Then pops out of his burrow,
And doesn't make a sound.

He can't predict the weather
As some folks often say.
But I'll predict, if he is near
He'll never go away.

The name woodchuck comes from a *Cree* Native American word, wuchak, which was used to identify several different animals of similar size and color.

If alarmed, a woodchuck gives a loud, sharp whistle. When upset, it chatters, hisses, squeals and growls.

Woodchucks like to live alone. They hibernate in burrows for the winter.

A woodchuck is also known as the groundhog and despite having a day named for it, it cannot predict when winter will end.

YOUNG

Woodchucks have a litter of 2-6 babies called cubs, born in the spring. The cubs are 4 inches long and weigh 1 ounce. They have no hair when they are born. Their mother nurses the cubs in grass-lined underground burrows for 1 month. At three months old they are on their own.

HABITAT AND OTHER FACTS

Woodchucks live in pastures, meadows and brushy hillsides. They dig burrows, 4 1/2 feet underground, in soft well-drained soil near plants and water. Their burrows have tunnels, up to 40 feet long, with several rooms and many doorways. Woodchucks can dig a tunnel 5 feet long in one day. They are active during the day from early spring to September and hibernate for up to 6 months in winter.

CHARACTERISTICS

Woodchucks are also called groundhogs. They are large ground mammals with yellowish brown to black fur, short legs, small ears and a bushy tail. Woodchucks are about 12-30 inches long and weigh 4-14 pounds. They move slowly, but if danger is near they hurry into their burrows or climb a tree. Predators of woodchucks are dogs, foxes and coyotes.

FOOD

Woodchucks eat grass, seeds, leaves, alfalfa, fruit, clover, daisies, dandelions, shrubs, garden vegetables and some insects. In early fall they put on a heavy layer of fat, follow tunnels to their hibernating areas, curl up in a ball on a mat of grass and hibernate until spring.

The Ohio Art Company, One Toy Street, P.O. Box 111, Bryan, Ohio, USA 43506-0111
(419) 636-3141   www.world-of-toys.com

HISTORY OF THE ETCH A SKETCH®

Its bright red frame isn't showing signs of gray. Its silver-gray drawing surface hasn't lost its shine. Its width still measures a trim of 9 1/2 inches… but the Etch A Sketch Magic Screen® is 30-something! It seems like only yesterday when the first Etch A Sketch® toys were produced on July 12, 1960. Here's the story…

In the late 1950s, a man by the name of Arthur Granjean invented something he called "L'Ecran Magique", the magic screen, in his garage. In 1959, he took his drawing toy to the International Toy Fair in Nuremburg, Germany. The Ohio Art Company saw it but had no interest in the toy. When Ohio Art saw the toy a second time, they decided to take a chance on the product. The L'Ecran Magique was soon renamed the Etch A Sketch® and became the most popular drawing toy in the business.

In the 1960s, Ohio Art used television to advertise the Etch A Sketch®. The response was so incredible that the company decided to continue manufacturing them until noon Christmas Eve 1960. The Etch A Sketches® were then immediately shipped to the West Coast so people in California could buy Etch A Sketches® on Christmas Eve and have them for Christmas.

The Etch A Sketch® has changed very little over the years. In the 1970s, Ohio Art offered hot pink and blue frames. But people still wanted the bright red frames that were so popular. The print on the frame has changed slightly, but the inner workings have remained exactly the same. The screen's reverse side is coated with a mixture of aluminum powder and plastic beads. The left and right knobs control the horizontal and vertical rods, moving the stylus where the two meet. When the stylus moves, it scrapes the screen leaving the line you see. The knobs have changed slightly. The new shape has a different edge for easier handling and turning.

What makes the Etch a Sketch® so popular? It has influenced a generation of artists who have made a road for themselves to press; magazines, newspapers, and TV. The Etch A Sketch® Club often features these artists in its newsletter. The Etch A Sketch® Club was formed in 1978 and has an average of 2000 members, ranging from age two to eighty-two.

For the 25th anniversary in 1985, Ohio Art produced an "Executive Etch A Sketch®" that was made of silver. The drawing knobs were accented with twelve sapphires and a blue topaz. The signature at the top was even hand carved. After 30 years, Ohio Art made a calendar depicting scenes from 1960 and each scene was drawn by an Etch A Sketch® artist.

Through the years, many people have used the Etch A Sketch® for advertising of their own. A lot of Etch A Sketch® things have been made, like mouse pads, cards, computer screen frames, mugs, etc. Etch A Sketch® has received a lot of recognition and still maintains that same level of recognition. A lot has changed since the 1960s, but for the most part, Etch A Sketch® isn't one of them.